WELL INTO THE NIGHT

POEMS

ANDREAS FLEPS

Energion Publications
Gonzalez, Florida
2020

Cover Design: John Raux, @johnraux

ISBN: 978-1-63199-739-6
eISBN: 978-1-63199-740-2

Library of Congress Control Number: 2020952387

Energion Publications
P. O. Box 841
Gonzalez, FL 32560

energion.com

For the frail. For the broken.
For the unholy words, sacredly
spoken.

TABLE OF CONTENTS

*The whole creation groans and travels
in pain together.*
—Romans 8:22

*Without God, all is night, and with him
light is useless.*
—E.M. Cioran

*Where there is sorrow, there is
holy ground.*
—Oscar Wilde

Well into the Night

FOREWORD

I met Andreas in Belfast years ago. I was speaking at a festival that he regularly attends. We got talking about poetry and we haven't stopped since. For Andreas — and for me — poetry is a tool of survival, a necessary art. Form, metaphor, syntax... these skills are all serving the greater purpose: a page speaking of life to the doubting. The speaker in Andreas' poems is brutal in describing the sharp edges of survival. This is not despair speaking, though, it is knowledge. Sometimes I think Andreas ate some of the fruit from the tree of life, and he's spent his years writing about the complicated taste.

In *Well into the Night* Andreas Fleps offers poems to catalogue survival: of depression, of despair, of doubts. "I board up my brain; / the storm comes from the / inside" he writes. These are essential poems, reaching for new meaning in old mythologies, damning the mythologies that fail. He calls himself the "tortured and the torturer". In all these poems lurks a God — a disappointing God, a distant God, a strange God — a God who can't fit into the word "ever". Both the poet and the god have feet on the ground, a ground described in tangibles, metaphors, as solid and as it is moving. More than one thing is true at once, Andreas asserts, and in his poetry, he presents pluralities and possibilities for survival. As he writes in Me, Myself, And I: "Contradiction is in the contract of being human".

Pádraig Ó Tuama

MENTAL HEALTH QUESTIONNAIRE

Have you ever had suicidal ideations, and/or when
was the last time you had the inclination to kill
yourself?

What do you do with time,
when seconds become a countdown
to your end, and nothing else?

What do you do with time,
when your future gradually begins to recede
as naturally as your past?

Why have you not acted on these inclinations so
far?

My family—
I don't want to enter their minds
as a ghost with hells still alive
inside it.

Are you a danger to anyone?

Physically, no, but I have slaughtered
peace of mind inside my brother
and slain sleep beneath my mother's eyelids.

When was the last time you slept?

Each night ends the same way:
a gasp like lungs lurching
for a world with gentler air.

When was the last time you cried?

Today—
tears puddled in the sore place
behind the eyes that never stops
seeing.

Do you think you should be admitted?

Did you say ashamed?
I'll admit, I have been handcuffed to a hospital
bed twice now, and the restraints never came off.

Do you feel you will ever get better?

I fear the "one day" I was promised
will never know day one.

I fear all my thoughts have shaped into bullets
instead of feathers, where they could have known
a different kind of flying.

Have you ever felt your mind was in a good place?

I am a Matryoshka doll. The thoughts are in my mind
is in my brain is in my skull is in my head is in my
hands taking myself apart.

Have you been on and/or considered medication?

Yes, anti-depressants are legion,
for they are many.

Here, take this blue pill

2

so the sky can be blue again;
take this cloud-white pill like the Eucharist,
and it will save you.

Have you ever considered a higher power?

Is there a pair of eyes in which God
has not been dressed?

Have you ever considered a support group?

Does a raindrop feel less alone
even as it falls amongst the rest?

You seem to have all the answers, don't you?

What good are answers,
when questions have longer roots?

A Boy

There once was a boy with fulgent hair
and a smile so sweet, bees would land
on his lips like flower petals and drink
his breath. And his eyes were mason jars
of twilight, and fireflies illuminating
themselves from within.

Then the school bell rang and he took
his seat in Suffering 101. The boy
learned every bone is a wishbone as it
breaks, and what it feels like to crumble
under the weight of air.

His anxiety began to count every barb
on the wire. His depression wrapped
itself into a knot of agony and he felt how
many ways a life can twist, hurt, and
constrict the light tightly in a fist.

All day, night nipped at his heels.
All night, day pulled on his arms as if
morning was a dance floor.

He waited for relief, like a patient in an
overwhelmed emergency room.
The emergency room was his body.
There were no competent doctors,
so he writhed on the table by himself.

He hoped for salvation or the
strength to endure damnation.

He screamed until his heartbeat said sorry.
He said sorry until his mother's heartbeat
screamed.

As he grew older, he grew strongly insecure.
He secured shame in the overhead bin of his
brain. He began to self-medicate with lips.
He kissed women. He kissed booze-bottles.
He kissed everything except himself.

The boy made mistakes and mistook them
for his name. Regret was his pet; he was the
one on a leash.

His wounds became the knives
that birthed them; they sharpened
their tongues to gut every kind word.

He cursed God. His hands prayed without
him knowing. He hung onto family, faith,
and the future, and when he felt nothing was
left, he clung to that too.

He cried until he was called rain and was given
medication for it. His tears didn't age. He became
a man and laughed till pain's side split into a grin.

FROM AN UNKNOWN PROPHET

I saw the heavens transmute to dirt,
and the Alpha and Omega was humbled
by our throbbing, wondrous, and unmessianic middle—
eternity caught between Isaac's bound limbs; two crucified
thieves. The pale horse blushed at our touch, ate the apple
from Eve's unashamed palm, and there was a rapture—
it brought us even closer to the earth's breast.
We were thrown into fiery pits and our mouths baptized the flames,
and there were earthquakes because of how desperately
we trembled to be seen instead of judged. I saw sin
undressing itself and there were two chopped off hands
beneath waiting for the touch of the other, and the Good News
wasn't spread because it was already known.
There was sacrifice—instead of dying,
we lived for each other. For we so loved the world,
we gave our one and only bodies. There were crosses—
we used the wood to build sanctuaries for those
who bear the weight of holes. There was death—
we resurrected the living. Stones were thrown—
we made eyes of the welts. We wept. More than water
was turned into wine. The blind healed those who could see.
The lame taught the running how to sit still with their shame.
God wanted to show his face, but we had already seen it
in the sky that kept wondering if it should fall and the sun
hesitantly rising each morning. Exile screamed and wailed
for home. Home asked, *Why are you yelling so loud?*
I am always here. There was wilderness—we planted tenderness
like trees and drank the sap with a hummingbird's urgency.
Prayers converted to action. The sea didn't part, but tribes
came together, and the Tower of Babel was built past the reach
of the Lord's anger. Love was like the oceans—seamless.
There were floods—we constructed arks for each other;

hammered nails into cheeks to save the two corners of a smile,
and the first murderer was the first to know forgiveness.
The Lord breathed into us, and we breathed him out,
and light was created to bless the dark, not erase it.
We drank from the abyss—drowned our empty centers
with holy water. In the beginning, we sang to and through
our end.

HANG IN THERE

Some have their heads in the clouds.
Others have the clouds in their heads.

I am told to hang in there as if they
don't know the ending to a leaf's story

or how sweet fruit has fallen into a
bruise or the numberless flowers whose

skulls weigh too much for their bodies
to hold up, so they droop like a scolded

dog, turning away from the light. The other
day I saw a spider suspended in the middle

of my family room, seemingly swimming
through the air, though I knew it was hanging on

by a thread of its own making like everything else.
As it slowly climbed upward, I thought about the

dirty and fraying rope I had to ascend once in gym
class and I reached for the bell to make music from

my strength, and for a few seconds I made the heavens
ring with my hands. Maybe that's why I still try to write

my name in the sky with wounds and sweat and saliva,
and if I end up falling, maybe it's like two children on a

trampoline—how when one plummets, it propels
the other into heights neither had been—

8

How one falls,
and one finds.

FROM GENESIS

revelation is all that's left. How we are perplexed ghosts
trying to cut out holes for eyes in the veils which
cover us. How I thought the Body of Christ would
be kinder to the body, but if life is an inevitable confession,
why are we surprised that our lives are such sorry things?
How certain churches are built with matches and turn
themselves into a hell trying to illuminate the Lord's face,
and faith is a bubble balancing on the tip of a sword;
how bursting is our common language. How we are nailed
to a cross beneath our skin, and Jesus cured a blind man,
but it wasn't so the healed could see the healer. How there is a
colossal silence that cannot be silenced, but with God's absence,
we have no shoes to fill but our own. Who hasn't seen the world
through the eyes of Job? With loss stacked upon loss and the
con inside consolation and how sadness skins you of the love
of your skin. There are seconds that undress us down to our souls,
and even though vulnerability is as colorful and ornamental as
Joseph's coat, it's the one we tend to leave in the back of our
closets. How God's lips are dry without our tongues, and a voice
is something that carries the hush of the innumerable dead—
heavy because of its weightlessness. When a teardrop falls
from its creator, it's towards all of creation, and when a head
bows, it brings your focus closer to the dirt and dust and ash of our
gradual parting. How Lot's wife looked back upon the smoldering
of her life like we all do, and how she is nameless because no one
called out for her. How it's more important to be a baptismal
making mercy out of thin air, and I learned the tomb was empty
because I can feel empty of God too, and look at all these gaping
wounds with boulders in front of them that could be moved by
the force of a kiss. Half of our story is written in the ruins,
while the other half will be written in what we make of them.
And maybe one brisk evening when a group of friends

10

are sipping on some rare whiskey, standing around a bonfire spilling their hearts out, the flames will once again think they are alive, giving commandments to the burning.

For Elliot and Kevin

TELL ME A STORY

Tell me a story about a string of losses, like a necklace of
pearled emptiness, or how another 24 hours is a beautiful eye
color. Tell me a story about the woman who was swallowed by a
dragon and chose not to become more fire, or about the tree that
was disappointed in the leaf that fell first. Tell me a story
about how all you need is a streetlight and a puddle to make
a star bloom from the pavement, or what it feels like to be
wounded from head to toe in skin. Tell me a story of broken
windows and wind breathing through them, and cracks like
rivers of light, or the one about aching feet walking beyond
their bones. Tell me a story about dawnings and how they often
bring more night in their hands, or how coffins only know how to
hug what's placed in their arms. Tell me a story about skeletons
and the heavens in their closets, or about a wolf in sheep's
clothing, who disowns its fangs and chews on grass like guilt.
Tell me a story about the man failing his way up a mountain,
or about overdosing on teardrops. Tell me a story about light
bulbs who like the dark better, or how the rained on shimmer
in the littlest of light. Tell me a story about the violin with no
strings that believed symphonies were left inside it, or the
history of lips and everything they forgot to kiss. Tell me a story
about the bottom of a bottle and bottom of a burdened body and
bottomless air, or how bombs have thought they could sing as
softly as rain. Tell me a story of cliffs and how they are
perfect for sightseeing or jumping from, or the one about
worship and the warships it welds. Tell me a story about
knuckles and regret and how the best punches always land
on the one who threw them, or of the stars in the sky, ocean,
and at the ends of our wrists. Tell me a story about the boy
who carried his body to his mother and showed her how he
spilled his life, or about candy and choking on hardened sugar.
Tell me a story. Fill me with word after word, and I'll tell you

where the period goes—but if I place it too early because I'm scared, tell me a story about what it means to be erased, or how to rescue an ending from its conclusions.

A SONG FOR THE BREATHLESS

God wanted to be praised,
and we gave it to him for a while,
until what we were praising grew
into something much larger, and
it was Love and it was Compassion
and it was Understanding and it
was Justice and it was Equality—
so we began to sing to each other.

O, we lifted every ignored, dark
crevice to the light. Told every
valley to stand to its feet. God
wanted to be praised—so we
made hymns out of the voiceless,
and stones opened their silenced
mouths to receive their due and
dust felt the gravity of its tongue.

We suffer ourselves deep down
into the heart of the world to hear
a new heartbeat, and just as Jesus
multiplied food for the hungry masses,
we must multiply breath for all those
who cannot breathe.

SALVAGE

For Maria

Blank faced in the face
of all that's blank.
Fortune-less fortune cookie
broken and mute.

God's blueprint shredded
into the sky.
Reasons shrug their
broad shoulders.

Does beauty come from the loss or for it?

Does it emerge from a tomb like Christ
or is it a rescue team deployed after a disaster?

Maybe beauty arrives to salvage what's left
because often what's left is all there is to save.

I've glimpsed how beauty lives quietly among
the ruins and the ruined, how it plants flowers in cracks
until they're gardens; breathes remains into poems
because grace isn't fussy, doesn't boast. It simply
continues to lend circumference to compassion.

O elegant elegy. O burning bow-tie. O top-hat
for rock-bottom. O painful years worn handsomely.

An ache is at the center of me
and beauty surrounds it.

Light reaches through space and winter
and windows and eyelids to coddle something
shivering alone like a suicidal thought.

O goodness and joy and awe and warmth
with hands like mountaintops—
come down to conquer
my rugged heart.

MUSIC FOR CLOSED EARS

Another day of going from field to field
looking for sunflowers to lullaby back
underground.

I am not of sound mind or body.

Worn, I lie in bed with the night
like pieces of a guitar that got
slammed on stage after a metal concert,
wondering how the death of music is
not silence but being silenced.

When I cannot sleep, I imagine the night
filling birds with songs of praise and perseverance
to be released before the dawn,
so the dark can fall asleep to a small blessing;
a tiny chested chorus of feathered saints.

Tomorrow morning, my mom will put water
in her grey kettle, and its insides will boil
until I don't know if its screaming or singing.

I am not of sound mind or body,
but maybe like a raindrop, when I fall to the
ground, I worship as I burst.

Maybe my scorched chords will not rise
from the ashes, but bring them with,
and I will adorn them with a shoreline mouth
and oceanic tongue.

When not watered from above, roots must
reach deeper into their lack to find life.

Maybe the sunflowers will forgive me
when I turn my throat into a flower pot,
have their roots touch my toes,
and tell the yellow notes to soar up,
up, but not too far away.

PSALM OF THE LOST SHEEP

It is a lengthy and capital punishment
This sensing you and not finding you
This finding you and not sensing you.
                    —Lluís Roda

1 Lord, what are you
but muffled voices
in distant rooms?

What are you
but a feast for the eyes
no eyes can consume?

2 We break bread
for our breaking
and share wine for everything
we won't be saved from.

Is darkness digested through
our gathered stomachs?

3 Is love the hell you created
so flames could scrape away
a speck of the darkness?

Do we bear each other's burning
so light can exist?

Or is our hell all this shame settled
in our bodies, which says forgiveness
ran out long before we needed it?

We grow into the flames
like hand-me-down hells;
does damnation begin at
conception?

Was Nietzsche right when he said
"you too have your hell,
and it's your love for us?"

Do your teardrops go by our names?
Do our teardrops go by your names?

4 Lord, the cup we want to be
passed from us is always the one
which finds our lips.

The thorn in our sides
isn't a thorn after all,
but the same old skin
continuing to hold us together,
life stinging through it.

What bent nails we have made of our bodies
hammering them into the earth.

5 Lord, our skies will never
be as blue as Valium.

Because of depression
we have made our beds in the depths.

Won't you come lie next to us
under the comforter made of

suffocation, bloody sweat, and Promise Lands,
which no longer seem promising?

Do you know where to find us?

We are in the rose petals pressed into
rosary beads, untouched by fingers
in prayer.

6 Did you think we would fall for it?
You made tears dense with salt,
so when our wounds are wept in,
the sting hides your leaving.

7 Lord, we sit in the dark
on the side of the road where many
travelers have been beaten.

Our eyes blink like hazard lights.

We let out long breaths
like a popped tire leaking air.

We all need help, but our eyes
are rarely pointed at each other,
and where our hands aren't,
yours will never be.

8 Lord, you spat and drew in the dirt,
but we were already on the ground
trying to make angels in the dust
like children in a fresh dusting of snow.

9 It doesn't matter if we plead to you gently
or strike you in anger—you are a stone;
you are waterless.

10 We have strung the harp of King David
with our burning; we play it
with all our fumbling fingers.

Do you know what's harder
than walking on water?
Continuing to walk on the ground
beneath our feet.

POSSIBILITIES

Build around this loss a land of the living,
plant a forest around a fallen tree.

Weave a world of all these wounds,
and command it to spin.

Exchange gifts with exile.
Reek of the earth's blooms and extinction.

Lend skin to God's absence.
Awaken this God that's never known sleep.

Revive survival, sew a spark in its eyes
larger than despair.

Hold all this earth, both tenderly and trembling.

Bless every inch of the middle
of nowhere with aching feet.

Serenade the shadows,
hem a spine between
a sore star's shoulder blades.

Chisel the reachable nothingness
into a communion wafer.

Kiss the weight of the world
on the forehead.

Wash the feet of meaninglessness
with tears and hair as it kicks the
breath out of your lungs, but not the
love.

A DREAM OF REVERSALS

This morning I woke up in order to dream through
unstained eyes. The pen that could only write *exit*,
started to write *exist* instead. Those that were weeping
were watering their bodies so they could flower
past their fingertips, and gardens of empathy didn't
know where they ended or began. Bees flew back to the
hour of their deaths and gathered up all their stingers.
Knuckles retraced their steps. Torn off finger-
nails found their torturers and kissed them on
the lips. A hatchet buried its head in the ground
and waited for its handle to sprout. Borders
crossed themselves out. Skin sang to its ghosts.
Bullets bolted from the holes they had made and
triggers refused to be pulled. War surrendered.
Every noose closed its mouth like a child refusing to eat.
Car crashes spread apart like an accordion and music
replaced the sound of wreckage. The debris of
bombed-out buildings danced back into place.
Hurtful words pressed rewind and went back
to the time before a brain thought it was a throne.
Terrified eyes bloomed into nothing, and there was
clarity. Dust accepted its dust—eternity converted to
this and this and this. The broken realized they
had more room in them for the breaking. Shrapnel
made pilgrimages to the holy places it had ripped
through. Trauma went to therapy and learned to be
gentle with its long, troubled history. Storms learned
to take a deep breath and became the calm before their
name. Fallen leaves ran back into the arms of their
branches—they realized leaves upon the same tree
may have differing opinions of the sun. Loneliness
was no longer passed around like a hot potato, and

people stopped lying about how their emptiness didn't burn. Kindness was a fact because death was still a fact, and the earth stopped believing in heaven so it could become one. I then opened the blinds in my room and everything was warming its hands over the combustion of me.

WHAT IS THE BODY?

And your very flesh shall be
a great poem...
      —Walt Whitman

the body is the longest of longings / to be tasted
and not be just a bite / it's a prayer, a wish, a fact
down on its knees heaving the weight of a breath /
a tongue in the mouth of every question / the body
can be a refuge from other bodies / it can refute
meaninglessness with the gentle caress of a hand
on a face / how a crescent moon tenderly cups all
the darkness / it can be an outcry or cried out music /
it's grief and the thing worth grieving / a door open
for a little while / then closed forever / the body is
what looks for its reflection in a puddle of its sweat /
the dust and the broom / handfuls of loss and dirt /
stars and laughter / it wonders / why shouldn't we be
handing ourselves over to each other like bouquets
of flowers / both colorful and wilting / the body is
what helps make the world as the world never
ceases unmaking us / it lives in its thoughts / like
a shell at the bottom of the ocean lives in its voice /
it's where a teabag of teardrops steep into a cup of
sorrow / some have blood on their hands / but everyone
has blood in their hands which is equally as violent /
it's flesh made word / a thought teetering on the edge
of a razor / it's a pattern looking for patterns to pat it
on the head / it's the gasoline and the match and the
extinguisher / it can be an ashtray where light is
stubbed out / be dressed in damnations even though
there are kinder ways to wear burden / it's what
glimpses the stars / gazing from one dark into another /

the body is an oil-less lamp persisting well into the night /
it's a bundle of bravery and despair / if you want to
make it dance / you better take all of it into your hands

TRANSCENDENCE

The sky's thumb presses on me like a child's
on an ant. Shame turns a whole body into a migraine,

and even numb hells are still on fire; lack of feeling
is a different kind of burning.

It's strange, how I am married to this skin,
yet didn't exchange any vows.

Every time I say the word *burden*, I want to stop
at the sound of *bird*, and tell it to fly as far away

from my mouth as fast as it can. Names and dates
gather like razor blades beneath my skin,

but sometimes they melt into silver teardrops—
weeping for joy because they aren't sharp anymore.

And for the briefest of moments the chip on my
shoulder grows stained-glass wings, and I swear

what weighs me down begins to worship all the air
beneath every butterfly. My heavy thoughts flitter,

and I dance without moving an inch; float without
leaving the ground—transcendence between every

tired toe—reminded that I do not believe in forever,
but being ever for the brevity that breaks our hearts in

two.

SHOW ME

Show me hands that can't be
hospital beds, or arms that haven't
been straitjackets. Show me church
bells sealing their mouths, refusing
to sing for what's said beneath them,
or hearts like honeycombs, littered
with holes and sweetness and the buzz
of what's yet to be made. Show me
wings that aren't useless inside a body,
or a voice that isn't an auditory candle.
Show me a tree that can bend and not
break when picking up its years of fallen
leaves, or roots that don't believe
darkness can be inched through. Show
me a brain where joy went to hibernate
and forgot to wake, or a birdhouse that
doesn't mind only being a home to a gust
of wind. Show me a garden gnome that's
content spending its entire life in the
motion it was carved in, or a fountain's
trickle not caring how it can only ever
imitate the sound of a river's purpose.
Show me a hello that hasn't been said
from one hell to another, or a grave not
inviting life into its heart. Show me a fire
not hounded by its heat, or a baby who took
its first sip of air and didn't spit it out as a
scream. Show me crumbs that can be a feast,
or a skull that isn't both a sinkhole and
Holy of Holies. Show me undrowned thoughts
and drowned livers and how there's nothing
more filling than emptiness, or a heaven made

of foot bones, holding up what no longer
desires to stand. Show me someone living
not as if they are where sorrow will end, but
where a small ripple of beauty may begin,
or a rocking chair on a sun-warmed deck
continuously nodding yes in agreement with life
for no good reason at all.

SURVIVAL IN FRAGMENTS

I had wished the happiest place on earth
would be anywhere that's beneath my feet,
but when you wish upon a star
the sky has been known to laugh.

I am tired of sweeping deserts with my tongue
and force-feeding my feet with steps
that are indigestible.

The entirety of light can be drowned
in something as small as a mouth,
but a second less of death can save
an entire life.

I have heard the river's sigh;
it can drown every voice
but its own.

I've tried to disinfect this life with alcohol—

If I could, I would scrub this body
until there's nothing left to call
dirty or clean.

The ground is crumbling,
but what of the up-rooting skies
and the air itself
becoming quicksand?

I am like the tip of a flame
wondering how much fuel
is left beneath it.

Survival: disappearing as
slowly as possible…

I board up my brain;
the storm comes from the
inside.

Listen to the rain;
hear the symphony
the falling can make.

What good has this done?
Harvesting all these teardrops,
when every choice leads to a coffin.

Where am I going
on these treadmill
thoughts?

Nowhere,
except with ever greater
endurance.

For every end
there are a million
beginnings—

Life is hydra-headed.

A MEDITATION ON FEATHERS

Emily Dickinson said
Hope is the thing with feathers,
though mine hardly knows feet.

Every time a bird slams into a window
and it lies on the stoop motionless and
wide-eyed, as if it's still letting the shock
of the world in, I wonder if it died
instantaneously—in the moment it believed
it had more sky left.

I wonder if a bird's song reaches
into air it has never been.

I sometimes want to cover myself
in tar and feathers, to be the
tortured and the torturer,
though a murder of crows have told me
the darker you are, the more intensely
the sun warms you, like asphalt in the
mouth of summer.

I wonder if birds soaring as high
as their music is what sparked our
imagination into being.

Sometimes the sky whispers to my heart
to arise and fill it with the broken beatitudes
of a fumbling frame.

I wonder if all the fallen feathers in me
are assembling back into wings.

I wonder if branch by broken
olive branch, my body is becoming
a peaceful nest for my soul.

EVERGREEN

Outside my bedroom window,
there's a dying Evergreen
the same age as I am,
weeping sap the color of my ghosts.

"Ever" is a short word
an entire life can't define.

"Ever" is a short word
God can't cram himself into.

I imagine its rings limping into formation
inside its trunk, slower and slower, like cells
with a cane. The tree knows, like us, how years
are both cruel and worth counting.

What started as a seed of unrest and willingness;
what grew into an elegant green dress for
fragrant dancing is now a desert's spinal column.
The tree knows, like us, how life is a long,
confusing kiss goodbye.

But hope…with its roots and mud
and heightening and dwindling and
breathing and choking—
even when it's a corpse, breath moves
through it and against all odds,
becomes our air. The tree knows, like us,
to never stop striving for life.

In this ritual of decay,
we briefly fill a moment
and moments fill an eternity,
and where one line of sight ends,
another begins, like branches writing
beautiful sentences through
God's bruised fingerprint,
in every direction imaginable.

ME, MYSELF, AND I

Do I contradict myself?
Very well then I contradict myself,
(I am large, I contain multitudes.)
        —Walt Whitman

Me: It's terrifying—how lost a person can get
        in the distance between two ears.

Myself: Everyone talks of the light at the end of the tunnel
        but what about the tunnel at the end of all light?

I: The pain was unendurable—eyes clenched into a cocoon.
    But I swear, when I opened them again,
    butterfly wings were emerging from the hells
    behind my forehead.

Me: If we were to decorate hell
        who knows what flames we could live with?

Myself: The only difference between dragons and daffodils
        is what they do with the color of a sun.

I: Does sandpaper dream of being silk?
    Do deserts have their own mirages?

Me: Are a monster's teeth always sharp?

Myself: Umbrellas are useless if the rain is rising
        from puddles you thought you had skipped over.

I: If when being born we could dip our toes
    into the air like we do a pool,
    would any of us still leap into existence?

Me: A bee dove into my black coffee one morning.
    Perhaps it wanted to add its knowledge of sweetness
    to the darkness.

Myself: The winter is too long, said the tree
    who had forgotten all its rings.

I: Do you think anyone has noticed?
    My face hangs like a lost dog sign asking
    have you seen my sanity?

Me: The scariest place bones will ever be buried
    is inside our skin.

Myself: Contradiction is in the contract of being human;
    each name is legion navigating its many.

I: We are stories learning to accept the stories,
    which can't be untold.

Me: Take the viol out of violence
    and choose to play a different song.

Myself: Don't let wounds become the only mirrors
    you see yourself in; they hold all of your trauma
    and none of your laughter.

I: Is quiet only screaming on a diet?

Me: Am I kindness or a tripwire?
    Should I erupt with honey
    or be disarmed of my skin?

Myself: I've burnt my tongue on every
        silver lining.

I: Does the wind realize it would have no voice
   if it weren't for everything standing in its way?
   Friction is its singing.

Me: There are controlled burnings and wildfires;
    my body is somewhere in-between,
    wondering if such distinctions matter
    as roots grieve in the darkness.

Myself: What is the longing for an exit from life
        but the wholehearted desire
        to find a more loving entrance?

I:

HERE

For Pádraig Ó Tuama

And we're afraid.
And we fear.
And we are hiding.
And we are here.
                —Pádraig Ó Tuama

Here:

Something tightly closes its eyes,
bruising what yearns to be seen.

    An ear opens like a blossom,
    listening for air to be filtered through
    dust's mouth.

The ocean can't change that it has a voice,
only the sound its voice makes.

    The key to kindness
    is being shackled, swallowed, or is busy
    unlocking all it was told it couldn't.

A breath is heavy with the weight
of each possessed pig cast off the cliff—
squealing with hell.

    A hug is being reached for and finds
    a sanctuary of arms.

Trembling hands fit together like a

universal puzzle piece.

A friend's voice squeezes suicide,
refusing to let it unravel down a spine.

Guns are loaded with unburdening.

An unfinished story
concludes with a kiss.

Scars keep telling their stories
until they believe in their own healing.

The word "next" is frightening
and necessary.

A god is hoarded in the hearts of the damned
and a devil is stored in the souls of the saved.

. Two exiles become one home.

Darkness is driving, but light paves the way.

The uncured are given the diagnosis of "Endure."

The grieving and singing meet,
calling the song "Skin."

Bullet holes are filled with water for baptisms.

Fangs are ground into granules of sugar.

Horns are erected in attempts to hold up heaven.

Bodies are blooming against society's seasons.

     Failure with all its uprooting,
     and failure's failure to prune a flower of its color.

Crucifixions are still not come down from
as the ordinary sky gathers around
the all too ordinary pain.

     A gentle man spits into
     the messiness of words
     and makes dirt shine.

Here: where a life is made,
undone, made, and undone again,
like a worn-in bed still warm from
so much lovemaking.

FLAMMABLE

Every room in the mind is on fire.
Doorways to hell and eyes like
furnished furnaces.

Choking on collapsing staircases.
Tasting each step that accumulated
to nowhere.

> The body can burn,
> but it's the psyche that's
> flammable.

The flames think they are spreading light
in a house with exposed wires, decapitated
neurons, and candles who disowned their wicks.
.

> Fires don't fill,
> they consume.

Sometimes when you wish for the sun
you get burning instead.

Sometimes when you hope for clarity
you disintegrate in your own purification.

Your brain is the homeowner;
when it wants to pack up and leave
it takes the rest of you with it,

and when it all goes up in smoke
it's as if to say, *This is what running
away looks like when you don't have
feet.*

What hurts more:

    burn marks
    or not being touched
    at all?

Who fanned the flame of a thought
until it thought it was the future?

    I know you wonder
    if ash remembers
    it used to have a
    different name.

DUST

To speak of joy
I must dust off
that part of my tongue.

I want to give a toast to the sky
but my vision has been scarred
by all the pain that dwells beneath
it—

Two feet on the ground
are the eyes of God.

Sometimes
when we dance
we sweep the abyss.

Sometimes
when we dance with the abyss
it ends up sweeping us off our feet.

My eyelids blink
over the opening of gun barrels.

Behind my weathered face
are cities of debris

and I ineluctably breathe in the ruins
of lives and futures yet to topple.

(My blood type is rubble.)

A building burning to the ground
is how it weeps for what it held inside

and what are ash and dust
but indestructible pillars of truth?

Though I imagine Jesus died with his
eyes as open to the world as his wounds—
imagining the miracles of
raindrops of glue
grass stitches
and healings as wide as any horizon.

It may be all dust to dust
but in-between we grew ears
to hear our gorgeously heavy voices
rising past the constraints of our lives.

Honey-breath
emerging from dry rot
thoughts.

Joy singing
through the ash
of a tongue.

PREDATOR AND PREY

...to be afraid of this death he was staring at with
animal terror meant to be afraid of life.
                                    —Albert Camus

Something inside me is being ripped apart,
and it makes me think of the time when I was
running on a beach in Naples, sweat and sunscreen
burning my eyes like two fiery pieces of coal in my face,
when I saw a mass of black caught between the onslaught
of waves and white sanded shore. There was a dead,
short-finned pilot whale glimmering like obsidian
or a punching bag drenched in enraged perspiration.

As I moved in for a closer look, I could see crimson blooming
in the gulf, and sea lions were tearing into the blubber like
starved maniacs, heads flinging back like whiplash, each bite
a scream for more.

When I started running again, I thought about how relieved
I was that the whale's eyes were already gone so I couldn't see
my end in them.

I also thought about the sharks that were surely on their way,
those radars of weakness and the struggling and the perished,
with their vows of never-ending teeth and insatiable hunger.

Something inside me is being ripped apart,
and if the body is a food chain, my brain is at the top,
and my barely beating heart is at the bottom, and dear God,
there's so much blood on my thought's hands, yet why do I
remember the skinny-legged, wild-haired palm trees as prophets
who never cease whispering of love, and the boundless,
blue sky open like a wordless book of blessings?

THE CARRYING

But this: that one can contain death,
even before life has begun, can hold
it to one's heart gently, and not refuse
to go on living, is inexpressible.
                                    —Rilke

Skin is an ark that doesn't know
what it's saving.

Are we vessels or urns?

The alcohol swimming laps through
our blood grows weary of tracing where
the pain is, and sometimes our hearts
no longer take pride in their shipments of life.

Eyes give witness to the tiredness
of witnessing, and hands carry in them
everything they couldn't hold on to.

The past doesn't know paralysis
and the future is already a ghost
deep inside the fabric of our bones
and how is it that emptiness can touch us
so gently we hardly know it's there?

Sadness causes the whole body to ache
and a smile can't heal a face and who knows
if the split-second silence in the middle of a song
knows there's more music left...

How many breaths can a corpse take?
As many as it takes to feel alive again.

And to those we love, say—

> *There is no tomorrow inside me*
> *I will not give you.*

A NECESSARY LIE

For Tom

Jack Gilbert said, *The heart lies to itself*
because it must... so maybe beginnings
and conclusions aren't as lost as we are.
Maybe I can convert to a smile even though
my face is devout to the sadness behind it.
Maybe light can make a nest of my bones,
or a teardrop with a heart stitched into it will
ascend like Christ. Maybe there's a little bit
of joy in the joints that ache, and a choir of
loss shares one mouth. Maybe eternal silence
will sing thank you in as many ways as it takes
to fill forever, and flames will forget what fire
they used to burn so strongly for. Maybe I will
be able to sing what it means to scream and take
pleasure in the building of a home as it crumbles
and kiss the ruins and let the ruins kiss me back.
Maybe trauma knows every inch of us, but doesn't
comprise every inch. Maybe existence isn't a bridge
between two nothings, and the body made out of
failing organs can be music. Maybe hate will someday
be homeless, or I can be taken into a different stream
of thought and bathed in it. Maybe my ears will be
rinsed of my pessimistic voice, and I will be air-dried by
a breath of hope. Maybe it won't be a baptism,
but I'll still come out new, and I will listen intently
to the glistening in another's eyes. I used to point
to the pain on my body and my mother would kiss
it, though whose lips will reach it now that it's on
the inside? Maybe it's you? Maybe we aren't merely
wounded giants trying to hide behind pebbles, and belief

isn't just escapism. Are these lies, if by telling them, we preserve a particle of the truth? I will lie to each morning in the name of my body. Command it to rise against all I know. E.M. Cioran asked, *What do you do from dawn to night? I endure myself,* he proclaimed. We endure the truth—the torture rack of our tongues—the admission we must never give.

AND

A beloved college professor of mine once said
"and" is the most important word in the dictionary
and I think it's because it's a bridge between two sentences
and it's a bridge between you and I and it's inclusive
and like a window it holds multiple stories at once and air is
just my breath and your breath and every breath
from the living and now dead circling where hope
is and I wanted a word that could hold an entire
life's pain and only a body can do that and when is
darkness not on its way and when is light not already
here and we say *there, there* because here is a hard
place to remain and the world is spinning our stomachs
sick and my eyes tried to be washing machines and belief
is bed-ridden somewhere between two drifting thoughts of
cause and effect and Lord help me and my mouth is
protesting each thought with silence and a river of
seconds is carving me out of my skin and the definition
of life has death in it and I am all out of tears and my
body doesn't know it so my tear ducts dry-heave memories
and the further earth hurtles into nothingness the more nothingness
there is to explain and account for and none of us know
our hearts by heart and look at all these shipwrecks
half-way to the bottom of the ocean casting their
anchors towards the sky like iron prayers and I wrote
my first poem in second grade and I don't know
what it said and I know what it would say now and our
eyes are always waiting to be seen and our eyes are
always ready to look away and when you scream
into the vacant chest of God the echo is your voice
running back to you and they say shoot for the stars
and there's only more burning there and meaninglessness
still has such kissable lips and my voice rolls with

54

thunder across plains of grief and my tongue is lighting
in a bottle and you can be chained to the ocean floor
and not drown like a buoy and I know all is vanity and
I still chased the wind and wrapped it around my wedding
finger and in the winter when the temperature is below
zero as if it's in debt to warmth the railroads are set on fire
and on burning rails towards a cold and bleak future a train
continues to carry what it has to.

NOTES

*Without God, all is night, and with him
light is useless.* — From the philosopher E.M. Cioran's
book, *Tears and Saints*

*Where there is sorrow, there is
holy ground.* — From Oscar Wilde's *De Profundis*.

"A Song For The Breathless" was written in light of and
shortly after the murder of George Floyd.

The opening quote to "Psalm Of The Last Sheep," is
from Lluís Roda's poem, *The poet said to his soul....*

The opening quote to "What Is The Body?," is from
Walt Whitman's preface to *Leaves of Grass*.

In "A Meditation On Feathers," I use a line from Emily
Dickinson's poem, *"Hope" is the thing with feathers - (314)*.

The opening quote to "Me, Myself, and I," is from *Section 51*
of Walt Whitman's poem, *Song of Myself*.

The opening quote to "Here," is from Pádraig Ó Tuama's
poem, *Deoraíocht (Exile)*.

The opening quote to "Predator And Prey," is from
Albert Camus's first novel, *A Happy Death*.

The opening quote to "The Carrying," is from *The Fourth
Elegy* of Rilke's *Duino Elegies*.

In "A Necessary Lie," I use a line from Jack Gilbert's poem,

Naked Except For The Jewelry, as well as a line from
E.M. Cioran's, *The Trouble with Being Born*.

In the poem "And," the quote I begin with is from professor
William George who teaches theology at Dominican
University. He's a brilliant teacher, and I loved learning from
him.

ACKNOWLEDGMENTS

A special thank you and deep gratitude to the following publications where three of these poems initially appeared, all in earlier iterations:

Two poems, "Hang In There" and "Music For Closed Ears" (previously "Music For Dark Ears"), appeared in the anthology, *We Don't Break, We Burn: Poems of Resilience,* Edited by Zachary Kluckman, 2020.

Passengers Journal: "Tell Me A Story"

I give thanks to:

My mother, father, and brother. Your love has held and sustained me. You encouraged me endlessly. Never doubted me when doubt took the place of my heart and pen. This book wouldn't be here without you because I wouldn't be here without you. I love you all dearly. Oh, and Lauren, you bring so much joy to my brother, though thank you for being my ally in misery. Cheers.

Mike Rigas. You ignited the spark of language in me, and its fire has brought me more warmth than you could know. I wouldn't be a poet if it weren't for you.

Josh and Melanie Hoeg. I didn't know friendship until you two came into my life.

Tom Van Houten. You are one of the best people I know of, and our friendship is priceless because laughter is priceless. You've made me feel a little more at home in this world.

Elliot Harrod. You're the type of friend that makes sure someone knows they're loved, and our conversations have blessed my life. You've championed my work and cheered me on. I'll never forget *Pyre* gave me my first poetry reading. I can't wait to see where that brain of yours gets ya.

Pádraig Ó Tuama. You are a kind and gentle soul, and it has been a pleasure to be your friend. You helped edit these poems. You made me a better poet, but more importantly, a better human. I will always be grateful. Your words bless this world.

My Wake family. You have all touched my life in different ways. Kevin Crouse (we've had some truly remarkable moments… cheers, mate), Lisa Mickey (you are a beautiful human), Maria Vaughn (you will always have a special place in my heart), Rob Zahn, Line Ivarson, Katie Pate, Tamara Rafkin, Monica Guirguis, Amy Higgins, Lucy Wadham, James Lock, Anne and Steve Priest, Bea Mariam, Maria French, and countless others.

John Raux. You are a brilliant artist. Thank you for wanting to be a part of this. It's an honor to be your friend.

Chris Eyre. You believed in this collection and my work. Thank you for making sure it was released into the world.

Pete Rollins, Barry Taylor, and Zachary Kluckman. I look up to all three of you.

Anyone with this book in their hands. Fight like hell to kiss every inch of this earth because it needs it; it needs you.

About Well into the Night

When overcome by the intensities of life, we often seek shelter from the storm in all kinds of impotent palliatives designed to numb and distract. Yet another possibility always presents itself. The act of standing in the storm. This involves enlisting the help of the poet. The one who is able to articulate our suffering in such an artful way that it is simultaneously sublimated. When confronted with the words of the poet, we can find a way to bear the intensities of life and even celebrate them. Andreas Fleps is such a poet. His work mines the darkest recesses of the human experience without flinching. Yet he speaks this reality in such a piercing way that it undergoes a reversal. Darkness becomes light, death becomes life. These poems penetrate the dark heart of human existence while protesting against hopelessness. Their exploration of the night bears witness to the coming of the dawn. — Pete Rollins

Andreas Fleps' *Well into the Night* is a gift made with trembling hands to the enemies we may see inside our own skin. A love note to the obstacles, this collection is celebratory in its revelation and accounting of struggle. Like a child dancing in the storm, naming the thunder while refusing to be cowed by its violence, Fleps' work here is remarkable for its daring. From the surprisingly delicate language with which he transcribes trauma to the depths of his narrative curiosity, Fleps reminds us how someone who has felt "the emergency room was his body" can also experience the call of empathy for others, to "... multiply breath for those who cannot breathe." These poems are an almost autonomic response to the experience of living. *Well into the Night* is a book that belongs on every bookshelf. — Zachary Kluckman, author of *Some of It is Muscle* and *The Animals in Our Flesh*.

I met the man before I met his words. I sensed his hunger before I dined at his table. In this age where people seem to be reacting to abstraction with increasing rage and frustration, and are grasping onto nostalgia like a raft in a storm — poets are needed more than ever. Those who can weave a new imaginary, call for a new future, pull us toward the uncertain without resorting to tired tropes and empty platitudes. This is a book for the hungry, for those who yearn, not for some reframing of what has already been, but a new world yet to be born, hidden in the folds of poetic license. – Barry Taylor

CPSIA information can be obtained
at www.ICGtesting.com
Printed in the USA
BVHW030805240721
612786BV00005B/121